# Every Day with Jesus
# Insights

*Anxiety*

**Janet Penny**

**CWR**

© CWR 2020

Published 2020 by CWR, Waverley Abbey House, Waverley Lane, Farnham, Surrey GU9 8EP, UK.

CWR is a Registered Charity – Number 294387 and a Limited Company registered in England – Registration Number 1990308.

The right of Janet Penny to be identified as the author of this work has been asserted by her in accordance with the Copyright, Designs and Patents Act 1988.

For a list of National Distributors, visit cwr.org.uk/distributors

Unless otherwise indicated, Scripture references are taken from taken from the Holy Bible, New International Version® Anglicised, NIV® Copyright © 1979, 1984, 2011 by Biblica, Inc.® Used by permission. All rights reserved worldwide.

Other versions used:

NLT: New Living Translation, Copyright © ©1996, 2004, 2007, 2013, 2015 by Tyndale House Foundation. Used by permission of Tyndale House Publishers Inc., Carol Stream, Illinois 60188. All rights reserved.

*The Message*, copyright © 1993, 2002, 2018 by Eugene H. Peterson. Used by permission of NavPress. All rights reserved. Represented by Tyndale House Publishers, Inc. Good News Bible (Anglicised © 2014) published by The Bible Societies/Collins © American Bible Society. All rights reserved.

Concept development, editing, design and production by CWR.

Every effort has been made to ensure that this book contains the correct permissions and references, but if anything has been inadvertently overlooked the Publisher will be pleased to make the necessary arrangements at the first opportunity. Please contact the Publisher directly.

Printed in the UK by Linney

ISBN: 978-1-78951-275-5

*In loving memory of*
*Evelyn Patricia Dunnings*
*(1936–2019)*

# Introduction

Humans have such a wonderful capacity for creativity and imagination. Although our bodies can only be in one place at a time, our minds can time-travel back to memories of the past and forward to dreams about what we hope for in the future. The shadow side of this means that we can also think about all the things that might go wrong, worry what others think, or find ourselves overwhelmed by fearful thoughts, anxieties and concerns.

Anxiety, in all its various shapes and sizes, is distressing. In addition to impacting our thoughts and feelings, we experience the effects of anxiety in our bodies, and as Christians we are certainly not immune to this suffering. As a Christian psychologist I have not only worked with many faith-filled people over the years who have suffered anxiety, but have personally felt its ripples in my own life. Yet in all this, God is with us. The Bible's repeated encouragement to not fear is a grace that points to His compassionate understanding of what we experience, and tenderness towards our vulnerability. He is profoundly with us.

As you take the time each day to pause, read and pray, you may wish to keep a journal and capture anything that particularly speaks to you. These thoughts can form part of your ongoing conversation with the Lord and be helpful reminders that anchor you in the times when anxiety threatens to engulf you. Through these readings, I pray you will know more of His love for you and His abiding presence with you always.

'Now may the Lord of peace himself give you peace at all times and in every way. The Lord be with all of you' (2 Thess. 3:16).

## ● 01
# All who are weary

**READ: MATTHEW 11:28–30**

'Come to me, all you who are weary and burdened, and I will give you rest.' (v28)

Anxiety, fear and worry can weigh heavily upon us and wear us out. For some, it's like being constantly on guard, waiting and watching for things that might go wrong. For others, it's the feeling in the body of never quite being able to switch off, or being overwhelmed by our own thoughts and fears. Even the most faithful followers of Jesus can experience anxieties in various forms. It can be distressing and exhausting, and lonely if others don't quite understand the pain of anxiety. With 366 encouragements in the Bible to 'fear not', it can feel a bit discouraging when anxiety seems to shout the loudest.

And then there's Jesus. He extends this beautiful invitation to us to come to Him, to learn to live a different way, to find a place of rest. *The Message* paraphrases these familiar words so wonderfully: 'Get away with me and you'll recover your life. I'll show you how to take a real rest. Walk with me and work with me—

watch how I do it. Learn the unforced rhythms of grace. I won't lay anything heavy or ill-fitting on you. Keep company with me and you'll learn to live freely and lightly.'

When we're anxious, the temptation can be to read these words as a formula: 'If I just pray a certain way, or read the Bible enough... then I will experience His rest.' Yes, these things are important, but it is firstly about who Jesus is. Formulas don't often fit well into relationships. We are to do our part in getting to know Him, but we love because He first loved us – anxieties and all. That is who we are coming to.

Trusting is not about whipping up some state of faith, denial or persuasion, but is deeply relational. It is when we say, 'God, I trust that You are who You say you are.' From that position, praying is very different. It is where we know the nature of the one to whom we come and ask.

As we ask for help with feelings that overwhelm us, let's ask from a place of rest and not anxious striving, knowing that Jesus extends His invitation to us out of love because He is love.

# A lighter load

**READ: MATTHEW 11:28–30**

'For my yoke is easy and my burden is light.'

We're going to stay with these verses from Matthew 28 for another day and look at the kind of 'burden' that Jesus gives us. Anxiety, worry, and stress will give us huge and heavy burdens. Worry demands that we look ahead to the future and make sure everything is OK, anxiety keeps us constantly on alert for threats inside and out, and stress is having more to cope with than we can bear. These burdens can be placed on us from others or the situations we face, or we may have grown up in ways that have left us weighed down. But, importantly, we can also be tempted to place them on ourselves. For example, having unrealistic expectations of ourselves can leave us painfully aware of the ways in which we fall short, and anxious about getting things wrong or not being good enough. This is indeed a heavy burden.

The Greek word for 'light' that describes Jesus' burden is *chrestos* – the word also used to describe a good bottle of wine that goes down smoothly. It is not bitter or harsh, but kind, the same word used for 'kindness' in Paul's list of the fruit of the Spirit. His burden is kind, not harsh. And the evidence we see of this in our lives is not only kindness towards others, but also ourselves.

How easy it is to give in to the temptation to treat ourselves harshly, carrying additional burdens that Jesus has not given us. We were not designed to take on more than He gives. Do you add to what Jesus has already given you to carry? We can become so used to carrying a heavy load that we don't really notice the burdens themselves, but are very aware of how we are left feeling. Ask the Lord to help you begin to notice where the conversation you have within yourself is harsh; what can you lay down before Him at the cross? Can you hear His call to carry a lighter, kinder burden?

Jesus, thank You that You know me and love me, and that Your invitation is to live 'freely and lightly'. Help me to see where I might be unnecessarily adding to the burden that You give me. Amen.

# He calls us by name

**READ: LUKE 10:38–42**

'but few things are needed – or indeed only one. Mary has chosen what is better, and it will not be taken away from her.' (v42)

I can't help but feel some sympathy for Martha in this passage – the preparations had to be made, after all. She was busy getting everything ready, while Mary enjoyed the privilege of sitting and listening at Jesus' feet. But we read that Martha was distracted, and 'worried and upset about many things' (v40). It was perhaps less about the tasks themselves but more how Martha approached them and how she was feeling. I wonder what was going through her mind; I wonder what it was like for her to feel anxious and upset with Jesus present in her home.

'Martha, Martha,' He replies to her frustrations. Jesus' first response is to call her by name. He knows her, sees her and understands that she is worried. He tells her that few things, or only one thing, is needed. We do not get told what that one thing is, but Jesus affirms Mary's choice to sit at His feet and listen.

Whenever this passage is preached on in churches, it seems common for people to be invited to consider whether they are a 'Martha' or a 'Mary'. The implication is that some people tend to be more practical and get on with things, whereas others are more contemplative or worshipful. But I don't think we should pit practical acts of service against being in Jesus' presence and listening. Both are needed. Whether you think of yourself more as a 'Martha' or a 'Mary', in your serving or worship, Jesus reminds us that we sometimes get distracted and anxious by taking on too many things. But there is no condemnation in this; Jesus starts from a place of calling us by name. He knows us, sees and understands.

When things are really pressurised, the temptation can be to work harder, to do more. But that's the point at which it is important to stand against the oncoming tide of concerns, albeit briefly, to stop and pause and simply be with Jesus – to sit at His feet and choose what is better.

Take a moment to pause and sit at Jesus' feet. Briefly name the things that are weighing you down, things that you are worried and upset about. Hear His voice calling you by name.

# Anxiety is normal

**READ: PSALM 139:1–24**

'For you created my inmost being... I praise you because I am fearfully and wonderfully made' (vv13–14)

Anxiety is a normal human response. We are designed to become aware and ready when something threatening comes our way. We most often feel it immediately in our bodies; for example, with an increased heart rate or feelings of alertness. It's the body's way of preparing us for action and telling us that something could be dangerous – a bit like the warning light on the dashboard of a car that signals something needs attention. How great it is that we have this inbuilt alarm system that protects us and helps us in times of trouble.

The Bible has many examples of people experiencing anxiety and fear. Moses was concerned about facing Pharaoh; Abraham was anxious and lied to King Abimelech about his wife Sarah; and Gideon feared for his life, to name just a few.

Like anger (also a normal human response), anxiety can become more problematic when the emotion dominates and overwhelms or lingers. As the writer of Proverbs says, 'Anxiety weighs down the heart' (12:25). Feelings of anxiety are distressing. Added to that is the potential for us to then feel guilty or anxious about our anxiety, somewhat trapped in a cycle of difficult feelings and thoughts of condemnation.

Returning to Psalm 139, we see that David was known by the Lord intimately. He writes, 'you perceive my thoughts from afar... you are familiar with all my ways... you created my inmost being'. There is nothing hidden from the Lord's gaze. David was certainly not perfect – a work in progress, as we all are. Yet he had the confidence and security in his relationship with God to draw near to Him. We read his prayer at the end of the psalm: 'Search me, God, and know my heart; test me and know my anxious thoughts' (v23). There is no condemnation here, no hiding or pretending, but a simple request that the Lord would continue to know him and work in him.

How might it feel for you to ask God to 'know your anxious thoughts'? Is there fear or guilt in being fully seen by Him? Can you rest in the knowledge that God fully sees and loves you?

# More than conquerors

### READ: ROMANS 8:31–39

'in all these things we are more than conquerors through him who loved us… [nothing] else in all creation, will be able to separate us from the love of God' (vv37,39)

When we encounter difficulties, it can be a natural response to wonder what we have done to deserve them. Particularly in times of struggle, the impulse is to search for answers as to why something has happened. Generally, we tend to think that good things happen to good people, and bad things to bad people. It is the implicit belief that the world is naturally just and morally fair. In many ways, this bias in our thinking helps us to feel in control; for example, if we behave well, on some level we believe we can protect ourselves from disaster. It can be tempting to adopt a Christian version of this in which we perceive all our suffering to be caused by sin, or perceive a lack of material blessing as a sign of our spiritual deficiency. The bias towards a belief in a just world seems to neatly answer the difficult questions in life.

However, Paul's writing in Romans 8 (and elsewhere) firmly counters this human cognitive inclination. His own life was fraught with hardships; the list of what he went through (2 Cor. 11:24–31) is not comfortable reading. He was often in great danger, but also had a deep and abiding trust in God's love. Romans 8 ends with a crescendo of conviction in the love of God: Nothing, Paul states, will *ever* be able to separate us from the love of God. These are words to live by.

Rarely does anxiety leave us feeling like 'more than conquerors'. It tells us that we are inadequate, unable to cope, vulnerable, at risk of harm or failure. It can also challenge our belief in God's love for us. The New Living Translation puts it like this: 'neither our fears for today nor our worries about tomorrow—not even the powers of hell can separate us from God's love.' Nothing, including our fears and anxieties, will ever separate us from His love for us. Receive that wonderful truth today.

Father, strengthen my trust in Your love for me. When my knowledge of Your love seems to escape me, come again by Your Spirit and lead me in the truth of Your Word. Amen.

# Getting real with God

**READ: PSALM 42:1–11**

'Why, my soul, are you downcast?... Put your hope in God' (v5)

As a trained psychologist, I want to encourage you that talking to yourself is very healthy – and biblical, it seems! The writer of Psalm 42 knew this. We hear him asking himself why he is feeling down, and then he urges himself to put his hope in God, but we can also hear his note of worry (v9) that God has forgotten him. Although the Psalms were often used in public worship, it feels like here we are listening in on a private conversation with God, in which the writer acknowledges all he is experiencing. Rather than telling himself off for those feelings, he turns himself to God. He is fully present to God despite all that is going on.

I wonder how he felt after that inner dialogue. We are left to guess as the psalm ends with a repetition of the question and encouragement. Things are not exactly neatly resolved, but there is an important note of hope that breaks through the anguish. Like many other psalms, this one reminds us that we can pray very honestly, and that God is not surprised by the complexity of what we experience. He is accepting of the many different parts of us that struggle, as well as parts that can worship and trust.

Anxieties and worries seem to fragment our thinking, perhaps taking us back to things that we wanted to be different, or forward into imagined, future catastrophes. The Greek word for 'cares' in 1 Peter 5:7 is linked to the idea of being drawn in many different directions. We can feel that when we pray sometimes. How might it be to pray like the psalmist from a place of honesty, bringing all of our fragmented pieces to the Lord?

What is your own inner conversation like when you feel anxious? Do you leave your anxious feelings outside of the prayer room, or are you able to simply bring them to God? Can you, like the psalmist, respond to the loving encouragement to put your hope in Him, your Saviour and your God?

Father, thank You that You know me and hear me. When I am anxiously pushed and pulled in different directions, may You be my firm hope, my Saviour and my God. Amen.

# Learning to listen

**READ: PSALM 85:1–13**

'I listen carefully to what the God the LORD is saying, for he speaks peace to his faithful people.' (v8, NLT)

We are relentlessly bombarded with voices, opinions and messages at all times – television, advertising, social media, friends, family, strangers, and society all vie for our attention. And church life can be no different. Anxiety adds to the demand for our attention, often in overwhelming ways with an onslaught of negative thoughts and worries. This can put our bodies on alert, sometimes leading to physical symptoms such as palpitations and tension. It can be hard to hear God speak peace to us above the din of our own anxiety. Reflect for a moment on what calls for your attention. Which voices sound the loudest? How easy it is to hear God speak peace to you? Are there moments of frustration when His peace seems elusive?

Listening is challenging. It is more than just hearing sounds but involves our whole orientation to the other person, an openness to who they are and what they are communicating.

Listening means briefly holding back our reliance on our own ideas. Sometimes, we fall back on what we think we know and do not truly pay attention. We often listen through the filter of what we ourselves are thinking and feeling, sometimes missing what the other person is really saying. It can be a challenge to hear 'peace' when our own thoughts are fuelled by anxiety.

But God's very nature is peace – Jesus is the Prince of peace, and His message to us *is* peace. Think about how you can develop your ability to listen to the Lord's peaceful voice. Take a few moments each day to be still, and ask Him to help you hear Him over your own worries. Listening to God is an act of trust and hope. He speaks peace to His people.

Pause to pray and listen:

'As I am, I come.' (Name what you are thinking and feeling as you come to the Lord.)

'As it is, I come.' (Name the things that are happening in your life.)

'As *You are*, I come.' (Bring to mind who God is – eg, strong, merciful, tender, compassionate, holy, sovereign, attentive.)

# Getting off the worry wheel

**READ: PSALM 131:1–3**

'I do not concern myself with great matters or things too wonderful for me.' (v1)

Worry and rumination are common ways of thinking when we are anxious. It's no mistake that the same word of 'rumination' is used in English to describe cows chewing the cud over and over. Unlike problem-solving, ruminative thinking is repetitive but unproductive. So how is it that we get stuck in these negative cycles of thinking that seem to lead us nowhere?

Part of what it means to be human is to try to understand our experience. In some ways, it can feel easier to think about what we are experiencing than to actually experience it. If we can just work out what is going in inside us, it might lead to a way out of the problem, keep us away from difficult feelings and give us a sense of being in control. This desire to figure things out is understandable, particularly if we are feeling distressed. The downside is that we can get stuck in rumination. So how do we exit the 'worry wheel'?

This psalm was written by King David, someone who encountered a lot of 'great matters' in his life. He became responsible for a nation and faced many profound challenges. But he had not forgotten how to maintain a childlike trust in his God. He knew how to let go of things that were beyond his knowledge. It is an echo of Psalm 139:6 in which he writes, 'Such knowledge is too wonderful for me, too lofty for me to attain'. He had no qualms about acknowledging the limits of his understanding.

This was not a mere psychological coping strategy, but about how he saw himself in relation to God; a child who was content to not understand everything but simply be in God's caring presence. He knew that, as well as coming to God in joyful worship or anguished prayers, he could come with quiet trust.

We too can look with trust to our bigger, stronger heavenly Father, knowing He is deeply trustworthy. We can find contentment and quiet as David did, knowing He is faithful.

Loving Father, thank You for understanding my attempts to work things out. I let go, I turn my gaze to You and lean into Your grace. Thank You that Your loving arms hold me securely. Amen.

# 'Yet I will trust...'

### READ: HABAKKUK 3:1–19

'yet will I rejoice in the LORD, I will be joyful in God my Saviour.' (v18)

Habakkuk has a lot on his mind: he wonders when God will answer him, when things will change, why things are not as they should be. He and the nation of Israel are facing serious issues. Finally, after a long dialogue between Habakkuk and God, we reach the familiar end of the book where he declares his resolve to trust in God. However, he does so with a realistic awareness of what could go wrong. 'Though the fig-tree does not blossom...', he writes, going on to list various other potentially serious scenarios. All the 'thoughs' he mentions – the things that are difficult – add a depth to his resolve to trust and praise God. Facing what *may* be does not deter him from keeping his focus firmly on the Lord.

I'm not much of a climber, but the 'yet' in this verse brings to my mind the image of someone climbing a mountain, sticking a piton into the hard rockface. The piton is a small metal spike that is hammered into a crack in the rock face which allows the climber to get a better grip on the mountain. This relatively small piece of metal acts as an anchor, giving the climber something to hang on to, and enables them to keep going. It can be the difference between moving forward and falling.

Those 'yet' moments in which we resolve to put our trust in God, despite the myriad of challenges or feelings that overwhelm, is like the piton being hammered into the rock. It may only be a small part of us that is able to trust God, but it enables us to hold on and move forward. Like Habakkuk, it can take us a while to get to that point of faith and resolve, but we can join with him in saying, 'yet I will trust'.

What are the 'thoughs' that you might be facing? What difficult situations weigh on your mind? Can you find a piton to drive into the rock – a verse of Scripture perhaps that gives you something to hold on to? Ask the Lord to strengthen your resolve to trust in Him despite all that you are anxious about.

●10
# Think on these things

**READ: PHILIPPIANS 4:8**

'Whatever is true, whatever is noble, whatever is right, whatever is pure, whatever is lovely, whatever is admirable... think about such things.' (v8)

Some years ago, I was trying to park in a tight spot in the centre of town when I noticed a lady looking at me. I immediately thought, *She must think I'm making a right mess of this,* and started to anxiously huff and puff until I eventually got the car into the small space. The lady then walked over to me, handed me her parking ticket with time remaining on it, and we parted with smiles and thanks. It seems she was looking to be kind, rather than criticise my driving. How easy it is to assume the worst.

No wonder Paul encouraged the Philippians to think about things that are true, noble, pure, lovely and the like. Perhaps he knew that what we dwell on can powerfully affect how we think, feel and behave. For example, if I took a group of people on a rollercoaster, some would be excited and embrace it as a fun and thrilling experience; others would be terrified, perceiving it as dangerous or out of control. Our thinking is powerful, and our tendency can be to focus on the negative at the expense of what is also good and true. Many of the things we face in life are far more complex and important than a parking ticket or a rollercoaster. Uncertainty and ambiguity can leave us anxious about what might happen. Difficulties and challenges do present the possibility of negative outcomes.

Take time over the next few days to notice what your thinking focuses on and how it impacts you. Does it tend to drift towards what is negative? Are there moments when it fuels your anxiety unnecessarily? Try to take Paul's words to heart and notice what is true, pure and praiseworthy, especially if you might ordinarily be less inclined to perceive those things. Ask God to help you in learning to see and think as He does.

Father, by Your Holy Spirit, show me where my thinking pulls me towards what is negative without my realising it. Teach me to dwell on all that is true and good, and renew my mind in Jesus. Thank You, Lord. Amen.

# Hope and fear

**READ: ROMANS 15:7–13**

'May the God of hope fill you with all joy and peace as you trust in him, so that you may overflow with hope by the power of the Holy Spirit.' (v13)

Although we can experience anxiety about many different things in a variety of ways, anxiety tends to be concerned with what is (or may be) to come. It is a future-oriented uncertainty: *Will it turn out OK? Will God help me? What if I can't cope?* We feel apprehensive about an uncertain outcome. And although anxious thoughts often come in the form of questions, they are usually accompanied by a hunch that things will, in fact, go wrong. Even when we say 'I hope so' in conversation, it is rarely optimistic. In contrast, actual hope looks to the unknown future and is confident.

Matthew Elliot sums up the difference between hope and fear like this: 'Hope is the opposite of fear; where hope is a positive expectation for the future, fear is a negative expectation for the future.' He helpfully goes on to say: 'A life free from fear is part of the hope offered by Yahweh. The ideal may not come to pass in the present, but it is a promise that will be fulfilled.'[1]

In Jesus we hope. This is not a flimsy hope that takes its chances, but something sure and solid that we can live by. The writer of Hebrews describes our hope as an 'anchor for the soul, firm and secure' (Heb. 6:19). As a ship is kept safe in a storm, God's promises to us in Christ keep us and ensure the good outcome of our salvation and so much more.

We do not have to strive to hope in God as if it were all our own effort. It is about who God is: the God of hope, the one who is faithful to His promises, the covenant maker. Paul's desire and prayer in today's verse is for an overflowing of hope – not just enough hope, but a generous overflowing and abundance of hope that will spill out from our lives to others.

God of all hope, fill me afresh with all joy and peace as I trust You more and more, not in my own strength, but by the power of Your Holy Spirit. Thank You, Lord. Amen.

# Filling in the gaps

**READ: ISAIAH 55:8–9**

'"For my thoughts are not your thoughts, neither are your ways my ways," declares the Lord.' (v8)

What comes to mind after you read each of these sentences?

*John reached for the sharp knife.*
*He was looking forward to his birthday cake.*
*Once surgery was over, he would be able to celebrate.*

As you read each sentence, did you think John was a murderer, about to cut a cake, or a surgeon? Our minds are amazing. It is said that humans have about 100 billion neurons in the brain, with 200 neurons firing per second, each being connected to another 1,000 neurons. That is 200,000 bits of information per second! Our minds have a great ability to think fast. When there is ambiguity, we tend to fill in the gaps – so you can be excused for first thinking that John was a murderer after reading the first sentence. This tendency to complete what is missing helps us process quickly, but can come at the expense of accuracy.

Humans like to avoid uncertainty, and when there is ambiguity in what we are experiencing, anxiety can fill in the gaps negatively. The body then reacts to the perception of threat, leading to more anxious thoughts. How quickly we can end up in a vicious and distressing cycle.

In Paul's wonderful treatise on love in 1 Corinthians 13, he reminds us that 'we see through a glass darkly' (1 Cor. 13:12, KJV). Our human knowledge is incomplete and imperfect. In contrast, we read today that God's thoughts are higher than ours. In Psalm 139, David celebrates the Lord's thoughts as 'precious' to him (v17).

When anxious thoughts prevail, we can acknowledge them with compassion, knowing God understands how uncomfortable uncertainty is for us. We can also hold those thoughts a little lightly, where possible, knowing that we do not always see the whole picture. Not knowing is a place of trust. Ask the Lord to be with you in your not-knowing. May He fill the gaps of uncertainty with a deeper knowledge of Him.

Loving Father, in my uncertainty, may I know the assurance of Your love for me. Thank You that You hear each of my anxious thoughts and care for me. May my trust in You deepen day by day. Amen.

# Receiving peace

**READ: JOHN 14:23–27**

'Peace I leave with you; my peace I give you. I do not give to you as the world gives. Do not let your hearts be troubled and do not be afraid.' (v27)

I have some friends who, when I greet them with, 'Nice to see you,' they reply with, 'It's nice to be seen.' It is indeed wonderful to be seen by others and known for who we are. We have many different ways of greeting our friends and family. In Jesus' time, it was usual to greet others using a phrase that wished peace on that person. This verse starts with the common salutation, but Jesus then goes on to say more about this precious gift of peace.

God's peace is a gift. It is not something we can earn. If you've ever given a child a present, you'll know what a blessing it is to see them excitedly open the gift and enjoy it. In that moment, nothing else matters to the child as they get stuck into what they've been given. Children know how to receive! As we grow older, a number of things can make it harder for us to simply accept what God gives us.

We may rightly think of giving to others before receiving ourselves, but we can also become self-reliant, looking for our own ways to try to find peace. God's peace comes in the context of our relationship with Him. We read in today's verses and the following chapters that God, through His Spirit, comes to us and makes His home with us (v23). The Holy Spirit teaches and reminds us of what Jesus has said (He knows we will need reminding!).

Sometimes it can feel as though peace eludes us, and we find ourselves seemingly far away from the truth of this verse. But our worries and fears can be what remind us to return to the place of rest – where Jesus is at home with us, where we can better hear the Holy Spirit whisper His peace to us again.

Reflect for a moment on Jesus' peace as His gift to you. What does it bring to mind? Is it something that seems far away or within reach? Pray honestly from where you are and ask the Holy Spirit to help you receive His peace in this moment.

# He understands our vulnerabilities

### READ: HEBREWS 4:15–16

'For we do not have a high priest who is unable to feel sympathy for our weaknesses... Let us then approach the throne of grace with confidence' (vv15–16)

I was once asked whether it made a difference to my faith that the God I worship is three in one; Father, Son and Holy Spirit. I cannot claim any theological expertise here on the doctrine of the Trinity,[2] but my immediate response was yes. Within the mystery of the Trinity is sacrificial love. The Son obeys the Father, the Spirit brings glory to Jesus, the Father loves the Son. There is so much more we could say about this loving dynamic, the life of which we are invited to share in. And God has come amongst us through Christ's incarnation – another wonderful mystery. Jesus knows and fully understands what it is to be human in all its vulnerability.

The anxious person is often only too aware of their vulnerabilities, of what can go wrong or their own sense of insufficiency. Reflect for a moment on the things that your anxiety is drawn to. With 366 encouragements in the Bible not to fear, it can be tempting to think that God is in fact condemning of anxiety. But that is not so. In Jesus, we know that God understands our frailty. Prophesying the ministry of Jesus, Isaiah 42:3 says: 'A bruised reed he will not break, and a smouldering wick he will not snuff out.' There is tenderness in how God reaches out to us. Gerard Kelly's exuberant poem *Rob's God* captures this: 'Rob's God doesn't shoot his wounded or blame the poor for failing at prosperity. He doesn't beat the broken with bruised reeds from their garden or tell the sick that healing's their responsibility.'[3]

The confidence we can have in approaching God is not something we have to find within ourselves, but is based on the knowledge that He knows and understands us. It is a throne of grace to which we come for help in our time of need.

Loving Father, thank You that You are present to me in my time of need. Thank You that in Jesus, You truly understand what it means to be human. Help me to come to You freely and confidently to find help when I feel vulnerable. Amen.

# Jesus comes alongside us

### READ: LUKE 24:13–27

'As they talked and discussed these things with each other, Jesus himself came up and walked along with them; but they were kept from recognising him.' (vv15–16)

In Luke 24, we find two disciples (Cleopas and another) walking on the road to Emmaus discussing recent events. People were saying that Jesus had risen from the dead, but they were confused, grappling with disappointment and rumours of resurrection. As they unknowingly tell Jesus about what had happened, they seem to bounce from hope to despair and back again.

I am sure I am not the only one to wonder why these two disciples were kept from recognising Jesus. Was it something in them that was oblivious to the true identity of their companion? We can only guess. Later in the chapter, we read that their eyes were opened to who He was as Jesus broke the bread and gave thanks. They recognised Him in the ordinariness and mystery of broken bread, just as we continue to do today. And then He was gone from them. It is a wonderful and puzzling story. How like

Jesus to not fit our human expectations.

These two followers of Jesus were not the only people to struggle after the resurrection. The disciples were frightened to see the risen Jesus appear to them, Thomas resolved not to believe until he had firm proof, and Mary Magdalene wept in sorrow by the empty tomb. There was such a range of responses to all that was happening. In these post-resurrection narratives of disappointment, loss and fear, perhaps we hear echoes of our own stories. And each time, Jesus comes alongside those who are disoriented and afraid.

Jesus brought the two travellers back to what the prophets had spoken, and reminded them of 'all that was said in the Scriptures concerning himself' (v27). In times of uncertainty or confusion, Jesus brings us back to solid ground. We can draw upon the Word of God to anchor us and recalibrate our vision. 'Great peace have they who love your law', writes the psalmist in Psalm 119:165, 'and nothing can make them stumble.'

Dear Lord, help me, like the disciples, to talk honestly with You. May I know Your presence alongside me day by day. Amen.

# He gives us comfort

**READ: PSALM 94:18–19**

'When anxiety was great within me, your consolation brought me joy.' (v19)

The Psalms are such a wonderful source of encouragement. We recognise our own human emotions in the writers' words and know that we are not alone in wrestling with anxiety. More than that, God welcomes us into His presence, even in our anxiousness.

When feeling anxious, a common impulse is to flee. We want to get away from what is troubling us. When under threat, humans have been designed for either 'fight' or 'flight'. (If a large, hungry bear is eyeing you up as lunch, it makes sense to run away as fast as you can.) Anxiety levels can be raised by much more subtle and complex triggers such as fears of failure, worries about the future, or threats to our self-esteem, but the flight or fight response is the same. Avoidance and the wish to escape are common responses in times of anxiety. Not only that, it is natural to want to avoid our feelings of anxiety. This can also affect our relationships, as we may feel discomfort in ourselves and assume that others will also find our anxiety uncomfortable.

In contrast, there is no fleeing or avoidance in the Psalms. Anxiety is acknowledged, and everything is brought to God. The writer of Psalm 94 is bold in expressing himself in the Lord's presence. He has the confidence to draw near to God and finds that God also comes near to him. There is no running *away* from God, but rather running *towards* Him. In anxiety, the psalmist finds God's consolation. His comfort, mercy, compassion and support sustain and bring joy, even in the face of great anxiety. His comfort is available in these times of vulnerability. God does not need our strength, but for us to simply draw upon *His* strength.

Reflect for a moment on how you respond to God in times of anxiety. Do you have confidence that He will bring comfort when you come to Him? Or does part of you seek to keep your difficult feelings away from God? If you have not already, begin to have a conversation with your loving Father about anxiety and ask Him to bring you the joy of His comfort and support.

# Perfect love

**READ: 1 JOHN 4:18–19**

'There is no fear in love. But perfect love drives out fear' (v18)

If hope is the opposite of fear, love is the antidote to fear.

Fear and anxiety are concerned with a sense of not being safe enough. Some people grow up with experiences that have left them unsure about themselves, others or the world around them. *Will I be strong enough? Will others hurt me? Will circumstances overwhelm me?* These fears can become the lenses through which we view life, ever looking and alert for things that are not safe. This tendency to forever be perceiving the potential dangers can be like a magnet that automatically attracts the metal. Although there is certainly merit in working towards having greater confidence to combat fear, often at the base of anxiety is an uneven sense of love and acceptance which needs transforming.

In *The Inner Voice of Love*, Henri Nouwen writes: 'The way to "victory" is not in trying to overcome your dispiriting emotions directly but in building a deeper sense of safety and at-home-ness and a more incarnate knowledge that you are deeply loved.'[4] It is love that displaces fear.

There is much fun to be had playing 'peek-a-boo' with a young child who does not realise that the toy still exists even when it is hidden. There is joy and surprise each time the toy is revealed because it is as if the toy exists once again. As development occurs, the child learns what psychologists call 'object permanence' – the understanding that things exist even when they are hidden. Sometimes, it is as if our understanding of God's love for us has not yet fully developed object permanence and we doubt His love when it appears to be hidden.

Just like developing children, we are all at different stages in our relationship with God and our understanding of His love. We can lean into the work of the Spirit in our lives to deepen the knowledge of His profound love for us.

Loving Father, thank You for Your love for me. Thank You that Your very nature is love. Grant me grace to trust in Your love, and may Your love displace my fear. Amen.

# Let your God love you

**READ: 1 JOHN 4:18–19**

'We love because He first loved us.' (v19)

Have you ever tried to change the water in a goldfish bowl? If the water is suddenly thrown out, the poor fish is unlikely to survive the trauma. Instead, the bowl and fish are placed under the tap with the steady flow of fresh water pouring in and this displaces the old. There is little that the fish can do to help but remain in the bowl, under the flow of fresh water. Although there are many ways we can express our love to God – through service or obedience, for example – there is nothing we can do to make Him love us any more or less. He loved us first. That is the basis for our love-response to Him.

However, unlike the goldfish, perhaps we can do a little more to position ourselves to receive God's love. This might be as simple as asking for His help to receive it. It sounds simple, but many people find it hard to really know that they are loved by God. There is often a head-heart gap, in which there is a belief in His love, but less of a deeply held sense that impacts all of life.

Early experiences in life can profoundly shape how we experience love, and these are carried into our relationship with God, for better or worse. Thankfully, He is able to transform and transcend early patterns of relationships that have been unhelpful.

Slowly read Edwina Gately's poem, *Let Your God Love You,*[5] and receive the fresh 'water' of God's love that displaces fear.

Be silent. Be still. Alone. Empty. Before your God.
Say nothing. Ask nothing.
Be silent. Be still.
Let your God look upon you. That is all.
God knows. God understands. God loves you with an enormous love,
And only wants to look upon you with that love.
Quiet.
Still.
Be.
Let your God—
Love you.

# You are valued

### READ: MATTHEW 10:30–31

'So don't be afraid; you are worth more than sparrows.' (v31)

This is the second time in Matthew's Gospel that Jesus reminds us we are more valuable than the birds of the air. In Matthew 6:25–33, Jesus addresses the everyday concerns that we can all become preoccupied with. The worries of life that He mentions – such as what to wear, eat or drink – seem very ordinary and trivial compared to other issues that bring anxiety. Even small distractions and worries can weigh upon us. It is heartening to know that Jesus understands this. The birds are well looked after, and His rhetorical question confirms to us that we are much more valuable to Him than they are. We can rest assured that He knows what we need.

Theses verses, however, are surrounded by much weightier issues. The disciples were being sent out to spread the good news, and Jesus was instructing and warning them of the dangers they would encounter. They might be turned away, handed over for flogging, persecuted and betrayed – they might even face death. This is not comfortable reading. Yet in the midst of this, Jesus tells them not to be afraid. Again, He reminds them that they are worth more than the sparrows. Perhaps as the disciples heard this, they remembered that wonderful day on the mountain with the crowds when He began to teach them about His kingdom, saying, 'Blessed are the poor in spirit...'.

There are seasons when the anxieties and worries we face are considerably more serious. Even in such times, when Jesus says, 'Don't be afraid', it is not a baseless suggestion but a call to us to rest on the knowledge that God knows us intimately. We are greatly valued by God Himself.

It can be challenging not to fear. Attempting to *not* do something can ironically result in focusing on the action you want to avoid. Instead, people often find it more helpful to develop an alternative focus. Instead of fear, Jesus offers us the truth that we are valued. This is a truth to take a hold of firmly.

Take a moment to pause and bask in the knowledge that you are valued. Ask the Holy Spirit to deepen your knowledge of God's love for you.

# God-given rhythms

### READ: GENESIS 1:3–5

'And there was evening, and there was morning – the first day.' (v5)

Right at the start, even before humans and other living beings were made, God brought into being the rhythm of day and night. This is the God-given pattern of time within which we live our lives. The Bible reveals God as one who transcends time but also works within it. He invites us to pray each day for our 'daily bread', to see His mercies afresh each day, to mark the passing of time with celebrations and rituals, and, importantly, to cultivate a rhythm of life that allows for regular rest.

How often we hear ourselves and others wishing for more time, pressurised by what needs to be done. It is tempting, even within Christian contexts, to measure one's spirituality against levels of activity. The thought of taking rest can evoke a somewhat guilty feeling. We sometimes push against the structure of day and night – work and rest – that God has put in place. Anxieties can be driven by the need to get everything done, to work harder, to produce an outcome or stay on top of the to-do list.

Listen to how people talk about time. It is often thought to be the enemy that is constantly chasing us. In her book *Receiving the Day*, Dorothy Bass takes a different view, saying time is a gift from God. She says, 'It is within time itself that God meets us... a point of rendezvous.'[6] She also reminds us to appreciate the body's need for daily attention and rest. Honouring these needs is part of how we can love God with all of our being. Being attentive to the body and our patterns of rest is important in thinking about anxiety.

Return for a moment to the creation narrative in Genesis. We read in Genesis 1:31 that 'God saw all He had made, and it was very good.' Creation, including the rhythms of day and night He gives, is good. Not only that, we read in Genesis 2:1 that 'God rested from all His work'. The creator Himself rested. How much more, then, do we need to develop a rhythm of life that allows for rest?

Father, when anxiety keeps me alert too much and on-the-go, help me to rest. Grant me grace to live from a place of deep rest in You. Amen.

# Your body is a temple

### READ: 1 CORINTHIANS 6:19–20

'Do you not know that your bodies are temples of the Holy Spirit, who is in you, whom you have received from God?' (v19)

I've recently read that there are at least 50 million photos uploaded to one particular social media site per day – and no doubt many of these will be 'selfies'. The pressure to aspire to impossible and unachievable beauty standards is all around us as our culture urges us to strive for bodily perfection. Interestingly, we seem to talk about our bodies a lot less in Christian contexts. There can be a split in our thinking between the inner life of the soul or spirit and the outer life of our bodies, with the latter sometimes looked down upon or seen as something to conquer. But the Bible has quite a lot to say about the body. It ranges from viewing it as the place where sin can grow, to celebrating it and considering it holy – both of which are true. John 1 tells us that Jesus became flesh and dwelt amongst us. God took on bodily form. The physical body is not eschewed by God but honoured in the incarnation. How wonderful that God Himself in

Jesus understands what it is to have a body.

Anxiety often comes with physical symptoms, and taking care of our bodies can be really important in managing anxiety. For some, this may involve simple practicalities such as getting enough sleep or exercise to help regulate feelings. It can also be helpful to understand how the body responds when anxious, and the importance of breathing. Further to that, we can reflect on what the Bible has to say about our bodies. Aware that the disciples had no time to eat, Jesus said to them in Mark 6:31: 'Come with me by yourselves to a quiet place and get some rest.' He was mindful of what they all needed physically. His words speak to us today.

Take a moment to pause in prayer and reflect on your body as a place in which God's Spirit dwells. What do you want to say to Him? What might He be saying to you? Can you hear His invitation to come to a quiet place and rest?

# 22

# The promise of rest

### READ: HEBREWS 4:9–11

'There remains then, a Sabbath-rest for the people of God' (v9)

In Hebrews 4, the writer brings us back to the Genesis account of creation. He writes that as believers, we do not have to work for salvation, but we have the promise of entering God's rest. In the same way that God rested from His own work of creation on the seventh day, we too rest from the work of trying to get right with God, and by faith we take up God's invitation to enter His rest. The salvation work of God through Christ is complete: we do not have to add to it. 'It is finished', as Jesus said on the cross.

What an incredible invitation He extends to us. Imagine receiving an invite to a lavish meal: you arrive, but you try to get into the kitchen to help with the cooking, or you're anxious that you'll need to do all the dishes afterwards in order to earn your place at the table. How tempting it is to anxiously strive to be good enough or gain God's favour. Though we may work to serve God in various ways, we can do so from a place of resting in the knowledge that His salvation is complete and His grace is enough.

Ontologically (the nature of how things are), we are people of rest. This is what God has called us to do. Anxiety certainly does not feel restful. Rest means letting go of human self-reliance, instead taking up God's invitation and stepping into the slipstream of His Spirit. It might be difficult to lay down our sense of control or responsibility, but rest will renew and refresh us.

To what extent do you rest in His salvation? Can you become anxious about being good enough before God? Do you find rest in His grace, or is it tempting to slip into your own works?

Loving Father, thank You for Jesus. Thank You that You extend Your invitation of salvation and Sabbath rest to me. In all I do, guide me in Your ways of rest. May I more fully grow into a person of rest and peace. Amen.

# 23

# Where did you meet God today?

**READ: PSALM 68:19**

'Praise be to the Lord, to God our Saviour, who daily bears our burdens.' (v19)

Returning home after work or school, people are often asked, 'How was your day?' How do we tend to measure or evaluate how well our day has gone? Various things in the Bible are framed in terms of days: we are to ask for our daily bread, we can know His mercies anew each day, and we are to forgive before the sun goes down on the day. Dorothy Bass asks the question in a slightly different way: 'Where did you meet God today?' She writes: 'In the lengths and shade of this humble span of time reside regular opportunities to offer attention to God, to ourselves, to other people, and to creation.'

Similarly, Ignatian approaches to spirituality emphasise the importance of reviewing each day by reflecting on God's presence in our lives, and considering the moments when perhaps we were closed off to Him. Our day might be preoccupied by good and much-needed tasks, but how easy it is to slip into auto-pilot rather than live intentionally.

The psalmist declares that God daily bears our burdens. He does not leave us for weeks on end to carry a heavy load alone. Our part can be to come to Him daily, ensuring that we don't let the weight of worries add up over time without bringing them to Him. People say that it is important to keep 'short accounts' when talking about forgiveness. We can also keep short accounts with our anxieties and concerns, by coming to God regularly and leaving them with Him.

On a practical note, praying about anxieties can be harder at the end of the day. As we are praying, it can get sticky and leave us unrestful for sleep if we are tempted to problem solve the issues. Try to find a time of day when you can allow God to carry your burdens, and end the day peacefully without picking them up again. I find that the template below works well for me, and I invite you to join in.

One thing I am grateful for today is...
One thing that was difficult about today was...
The best thing about today was...
Today, I thank God for...

# 24

# God-reliance

### READ: PROVERBS 3:5–6

'Trust in the LORD with all your heart and lean not on your own understanding' (v5)

I am not someone who travels light. When I go away, even for a short weekend, absolutely everything is packed, and every eventuality prepared for.

Preparation looks ahead to what might be needed. Similarly, anxiety and worry look to the future, but instead, they anticipate potential problems and our deficits in coping with them. It can be helpful to adopt coping strategies for situations that we find difficult. For example, practising how to control your breathing when anxiety is high may help you in a moment when feelings overwhelm; or bringing a pleasant distraction with you on a flight can help keep stress levels down.

Sometimes, worry and anxiety themselves can actually become a way to help us feel prepared, in the sense that if we consider everything that could go wrong, we won't be caught off-guard. On the one hand, it gives a feeling of being ready, but on the other, it comes at the cost of being constantly over-alert to threats, forever in anticipation of the negative. Our bodies need time to power down, which is harder if we are always in a state of high alert. It can be helpful to reflect not only on *what* we can feel anxious about, but whether part of our anxiety is an understandable attempt to feel a little more prepared and in control.

God calls us to lean on Him. Letting go of our need for over-preparedness and self-reliance is not easy, but He has provided for us in all things. To let go of our own ways can feel like falling, wondering if we will be caught. I recently read a social media post by Gerard Kelly, reminding me that God's everlasting arms are beneath us (Deut. 33:27). He wrote: 'Into the broad and layered grace of God I sink. Into His great mercy I am folded. I trust, I let go. There is no risk in such a fall.'[8]

Loving Father, thank You that You are compassionate and understanding. May I grow in reliance on Your strength and power day by day. Give me courage to let go of the ways I cling to my own understanding. May my hands be open to all that You have for me. Amen.

# 25

# Keeping God in mind

**READ: ISAIAH 26:3–4**

'You will keep in perfect peace those whose minds are steadfast, because they trust in you.' (v3)

An anxious mind can be a scattered mind. Although our bodies can only be in one place at a time, our thinking can be drawn to fretting about the past, or full of concerns for the future. Being fully present in the present moment is something most people struggle with. Distractions pull in us many different directions. And even in prayer or worship, thoughts can drift towards things on the to-do list or things we are worried about. The recent popularity of the practise of mindfulness, with its emphasis on being present, is unsurprising given all the ways in which our attention is divided. People clearly want to live more intentionally without being automatically pushed and pulled in so many different directions.

In contrast to the fragmented nature of anxiety, a steadfast mind is unwavering, anchored. Importantly, Isaiah reminds us that a steadfast mind is anchored by trust in the Lord.

He tells his readers that 'the Lord Himself, is the Rock eternal' (v4). Imagine the anchor going down deep into the solid rock. In whatever way we are buffeted, we can remain steadfast in Him. It is not merely a case of practising techniques to focus our thoughts, though those these can be helpful. It is in relationship with the Lord who is deeply trustworthy that we can grow in steadfastness and know His peace.

The reality is that our thoughts do meander, like sheep that wander away from the flock, taking us into imagined feared scenarios or ruminations on the past. When they do, gently shepherd them back to God in the present moment. Return to a place of quiet trust and simply talk to Him about where those thoughts have been. It doesn't matter that this can happen over and over again, but, with time and with His help, we grow in our steadfastness and trust.

Lord, thank You that You are my rock, and that it is Your nature to be fully trustworthy. Thank You that You are steadfast in Your love to me. When my anxious thoughts are scattered, may I simply return to You again. May I be kept in Your perfect peace, moment by moment. Amen.

# 26

# He cares for you

**READ: 1 PETER 5:6–11**

'Cast all your anxiety on him because he cares for you.' (v7)

This oft-quoted verse is a great encouragement and reminder that God cares for us. The apostle Peter was likely very familiar with the Psalms and, in his letter, he brings his readers back to the words of King David: 'Cast your cares on the LORD and he will sustain you; he will never let the righteous be shaken' (Psa. 55:22). It is a comfort to know that, although separated by hundreds of years, God revealed Himself to both David and Peter as having care for His people. He is the same God throughout history who cares and sustains. Unlike the false gods of biblical times who were worshipped from a distance, disinterested and uninvolved, the Lord comes near to His people and cares for them. He is tender and merciful.

Our part is to cast 'all our anxiety' on Him. Whether big or small, our worries and fears can be thrown on the Lord. The word 'cast' only appears one other time in the New Testament, when the disciples throw their coats on the colt that takes Jesus into Jerusalem (Luke 19:35). It is an action that has some energy behind it, not hesitant or unsure. In the same way, we can confidently throw our cares onto Jesus. Today's verse gives us full permission to bring everything to Him. Imagine throwing every care you are holding onto Jesus, and letting Him deal with it for you. You would then have empty hands, ready to receive what He then might want to give you instead.

So what gets in the way of us bringing all our concerns to Him? Is there uncertainty as to whether God is interested? Or questions about His care for us? Are we tempted to hold on to worries and try to solve them ourselves? Pause for a moment and reflect on anything that might hold you back from casting your cares on Jesus.

Loving Father, thank You that You deeply care for me. Thank You that I can throw all my concerns and fears onto You. Help me, day by day, to bring everything to You that weighs on me. May my hands be open to receive Your peace. Amen.

# 27

# Living in uncertain times

**READ: DANIEL 6:10–16**

'Three times a day he got down on his knees and prayed, giving thanks to God, just as he had done before.' (v10)

There are times when events outside our control impact us profoundly. In the book of Daniel, Israel was exiled to Babylon where Daniel, along with a number of other Israelite men, was taken into the royal court of Nebuchadnezzar to learn the Babylonian language and culture. He was displaced from his own way of life into something very unfamiliar and potentially unsafe.

Wider social changes and events can upset our equilibrium. It is natural to feel anxious in times of uncertainty and change, whether on a larger or smaller scale. But Daniel seemed to flourish in his new surroundings. He both adapted and kept a sense of continuity. He learned the Babylonian culture, yet also remained faithful to God. We read in Daniel 1 that he resolved not to become defiled by the royal food, and he continued to pray three times a day.

A thermostat is designed to keep the temperature constant: if the door to the building is left open and the temperature drops, the thermostat kicks in to raise the temperature back to normal. Humans can be a bit like thermostats, in that we often work hard to keep things the same and find adjusting to change difficult. Change challenges us and tests our usual ways of coping. It is natural to feel anxious when things are unsettled.

When things outside of our control stir up feelings of anxiety and uncertainty, it is helpful to acknowledge the situation being faced. Psychologists agree that naming difficulties and the uncomfortable emotions we experience is healthy. Daniel recognised and accepted his new way of life, but he also continued to seek the Lord in his new home. He did not let his faith get shaken.

Name some of the changes that you are currently going through. What might adaption look like for you? Are there old ways of coping that now won't help your new situation? How can you remain faithful to the Lord in what you are facing?

Lord, I bring to you the situations that are outside of my control. Come near and strengthen my resolve to remain faithful to You. Give me wisdom to navigate these choppy waters and keep me safe. Amen.

# 28

# Sing and cling

**READ: PSALM 63:1–8**

'Because you are my help, I sing in the shadow of your wings. I cling to you; your right hand upholds me.' (vv7–8)

In a harsh desert environment, any shade is a welcome respite from the hot sun. In the ancient near east of biblical times, shadows were thought of in terms of shelter from harm; kings metaphorically provided the shade of protection for the people they led. Similarly, the image of wings is used in the Bible to convey God's covering over us. We read in Psalm 36:7, 'People take refuge in the shadow of your wings.' This is the place of protection and safety.

At the heart of many people's anxiety is a sense that life is not safe, and that, in the face of threats, they will not be able to cope. This might focus on a particular concern such as worrying about health or failure, being a good parent, or coping with the demands of work. Life can certainly feel unsafe. Events beyond our control can shake our sense of security.

It is so easy to respond to these difficulties with anxiety. Our impulse is to look inward to our own resources and see that we come up short when encountering challenges. But thankfully, the verses remind us that it is not dependent on our abilities or strength. We can sing in the face of problems because of who He is – our help. Not only that, it is His right hand that upholds us. In the Bible, the right hand signifies power, and to be at someone's right hand is a place of honour. This is the help that God offers us. There is a firm place beneath us upon which we can stand. So, finding a place of safety when anxious may feel difficult but is not complicated; we can sing and cling.

In Psalm 13, David expresses his anguish, wondering whether the Lord has forgotten him. It is his brutally honest cry for help in the face of possible death. Nonetheless, David ends with a note of hope, saying, 'I will sing to the LORD, because he is good to me' (v6). Although perhaps only just holding on, he clings to the Lord.

Lord, I so wanted the world to be safe. And it was not. But You are. I was made to cling to You. Amen.

# 29

# Waiting well

**READ: ISAIAH 40:29–31**

'But they that wait on the LORD shall renew their strength' (v31, KJV)

What did the butterfly say to the caterpillar?
*'It won't always be like this.'*

One of my abiding childhood memories is of being in a music shop with my dad while we waited for my mum to do the shopping. While we waited for Mum, Dad sat and played the pianos and keyboards – much to the delight of the shop owner – as other people were drawn in to hear the music. We can't have been there for more than half an hour or so, but at the time, it felt like forever. Patience was not my strongest virtue as a child! This is now a precious memory, but waiting is not always as easy.

Our whole lives are a kind of metaphorical Easter Saturday, in which we wait with hope between death and resurrection for the complete realisation of Christ's work on the cross. We are truly forgiven and saved, and there is a greater fulfilment to come.

Isaiah was writing to Israel during a period of change and national decline. He brought hope into their situation, reminding them that they were not forgotten, and encouraging them to wait on the Lord. Waiting here is not the desperation for time to pass, but a stance of hope and a time for renewal. We do not wait with passivity, but in continued relationship with God. The promise to Israel that comes to us is that we will find our strength renewed and our power increased. How we need that in vulnerable times of anxiety.

Anxiety takes time to abate. If a driver carries out an emergency stop, the car comes to a halt – but by the properties of inertia, our bodies continue forward for a moment longer, potentially causing whiplash. Physiologically, our bodies respond to anxiety immediately but take time to power down after danger. While we pray for change in our situations or anxious feelings, we can wait well, knowing that He will give us strength.

Reflect on the situations that you want to see change in. What is most difficult for you in waiting? How might you wait well? Take a moment to ask the Lord to assure you of His loving presence with you as you wait.

# 30

# And finally...

**READ: ROMANS 15:7–13**

'May the God of hope fill you with all joy and peace as you trust in him, so that you may overflow with hope by the power of the Holy Spirit.' (v13)

As we draw these reflections to a close, we turn once again to Paul's prayer in Romans 15. Repetition is common in the Bible. God knows we need to hear things more than once!

Although Paul did not write his letters using chapters, this prayer does come at the end of a section that focuses on relationships within the Church. Those who are stronger are able to support the weaker. He encourages them to not just live for themselves but to build others up and accept people just as they are accepted by Jesus. Whether anxious or confident, we are to love and accept each other. And if we feel ourselves to be vulnerable, we can know that God is mindful of us. Trusted others can play a part in supporting those who are anxious.

Almost all psychological theories acknowledge that humans are complex beings. We relate to each other, but also within ourselves. People reveal this when they say things such as, 'I'm very cross with myself', or, 'I'm in two minds about it'. Paul expresses something of this in Romans 6, when he struggles with sin within himself. We can have a mixture of feelings all at the same time – parts of us that feel vulnerable, and parts that seem a lot more confident. Although Paul is addressing a specific group of people in his letter, perhaps we can take on his encouragement to be accepting – not of sin, but of our vulnerabilities.

God invites us to push deeper into grace. His grace is sufficient for us (2 Cor. 12:9). In grace we face our weaknesses, our limits, our fragility, our vulnerability. The call to push deeper into grace is a call to let go of our abilities, our coping, our strength, our control. Jesus was crucified in weakness. The heroes of Hebrews 11 had their weakness turned to strength, and it is through weakness that His power is made perfect.

'May the God of hope fill you with all joy and peace as you trust in him, so that you may overflow with hope by the power of the Holy Spirit.' Amen.

# Endnotes

[1] Matthew Elliot, *Faithful Feelings: Rethinking Emotion in the New Testament* (Grand Rapids, MI, USA: Kregel Publications, 2006)

[2] For helpful further reading around the Trinity, I recommend Matthew Reeves' book, *The Good God: Enjoying Father, Son and Spirit* (Milton Keynes: Paternoster, 2012).

[3] Gerard Kelly, *Spoken Worship* (Grand Rapids, MI, USA: Zondervan, 2007) p15

[4] Henri Nouwen, *The Inner Voice of Love: A Journey Through Anguish to Freedom* (London: Darton, Longman & Todd, 2014) p34

[5] Edwina Gately, *There Was No Path – So I Trod One* (Naperville, IL, USA: Source Books, 1996)

[6] Dorothy Bass, *Receiving the Day* (San Francisco, CA, USA: Jossey-Bass, 2000) p11

[7] Dorothy Bass, *Receiving the Day* (San Francisco, CA, USA: Jossey-Bass, 2000) p31

[8] Gerard Kelly, *Twitturgies* (Maidstone: River Publishing and Media Ltd, 2011)

# Discover the full Insight range

Discover our full range of Insight resources and courses, all of which provide accessible and practical insights on tough issues that so many of us face in our lives today. The series has been developed to help people understand and work through these key issues, drawing on real-life case studies, biblical examples and counselling practices. Whether for yourself or to help support someone you know, we have one-off Insight books, courses and daily devotionals on key topics. Find out more at **cwr.org.uk/insight**

# These Three Things:
## Finding your Security, Self-worth and Significance

How do you sum up, in one book, content that covers our deep spiritual needs, personal motivations, and revival? Homesickness and belonging? Our disconnection, isolation and reconnection with God and others in our increasingly 'contactless' society? Let's start by going back to the original plan: who God is, and who we are; where it all went wrong, and how we find our way back; what it is we're looking for, and how and where to find it; all while daring to ask the questions:

- Who am I?
- Do I matter?
- What's the point?

Find out more and order at **cwr.org.uk/ttt**

**Free online resources available for groups and churches**

There's something for everyone!

## Find God in your everyday

If you love to spend time with God, then why not take ten extra minutes to hear from God and understand His Word? CWR's range of Bible reading notes include something for everyone, including *Every Day with Jesus*, *Inspiring Women Every Day*, and Jeff Lucas' *Life Every Day*.

Find out more at **cwr.org.uk/store**

Courses and seminars

Waverley Abbey College

Publishing and media

Conference facilities

# Transforming lives

CWR's vision is to enable people to experience personal transformation through applying God's Word to their lives and relationships.

Our Bible-based training and resources help people around the world to:

- Grow in their walk with God
- Understand and apply Scripture to their lives
- Resource themselves and their church
- Develop pastoral care and counselling skills
- Train for leadership
- Strengthen relationships, marriage and family life and much more.

Our insightful writers provide daily Bible reading notes and other resources for all ages, and our experienced course designers and presenters have gained an international reputation for excellence and effectiveness.

CWR's Training and Conference Centre in Surrey, England, provides excellent facilities in idyllic settings – ideal for both learning and spiritual refreshment.

**CWR** Applying God's Word to everyday life and relationships

CWR, Waverley Abbey House,
Waverley Lane, Farnham,
Surrey GU9 8EP, UK

**Telephone:** +44 (0)1252 784700
**Email:** info@cwr.org.uk
**Website:** cwr.org.uk

Registered Charity No. 294387
Company Registration No. 1990308